I0220735

The TAO OF DON JITSU RYU... The Unstoppable Force
Copyright © 2009 by Sensei Albert A. Andrews, Purple Dragon International and with the kind permission of Professor Don Jacob.

All rights Reserved.

Printed in the United States of America

1ˢᵗ Edition
ISBN: 978-0-578-01344-2

No part of this book may be reproduced without the written permission of the Author and Purple Dragon International

Publisher: Sensei Albert A. Andrews, 6452 SE Clairmont Place, Hobe Sound, Fl 33455
Website: www.purpledragonsoflo.com
Email: purpledragonpbg@yahoo.com

Professor Don Jacob: 151 Eastern Main Rd, Barataria, Trinidad, WI
Website: www.purple-dragon.com
Email: donjitsryu@gmail.com

Dedication

This book is dedicated with an attitude of unending gratitude to Professor Don Jacob, an enlightened teacher, motivator and inspirational spirit.

To the Shihans, Senseis, Instructors and Sans who live by the Tao of Don Jitsu Ryu.

To my Mother; Irma and Father; Richardson for their boundless prayers and words that still ring in my head and offer me guidance.

To my kids Michael-Christian and Zoe born into the Tao and Step kids Lana and Justin.

To our students who have joined me on this journey

And to Candia my love & life partner whose encouragement and support knows no bounds.

ドン流柔術

Written & Illustrated
by
Sensei Albert A. Andrews

Based on lessons taught by Professor Don Jacob 9th Dan

Founder of the Purple Dragon International,
Don Jitsu Ryu System and my teacher since 1978.

11/19/2005

Professor Don Jacob with our daughter Zoe.

THE MIND IS LIKE A
PARACHUTE...

"Long life"

IT ONLY WORKS WHEN
FULLY OPENED

DON JITSU RYU

begins

&

ends

with

RESPECT

A Sensei is
one who has
gone ahead
in life....
and is able to
draw out the
Greatness
in the
student.

In an argument the one who is considered more intelligent is always to blame.

So there is no need to argue, right!
It is ok to agree to disagree.

A

BLACK BELT

should not be angry

for more than

3 minutes.

(Professor Tom Nardi)

A DOJO

is a place where peaceful warriors gather to train and so gain enlightenment to take them through life safely.

Knowledge..
is like a cup
with a slow leak...

Keep learning!

It is <u>better</u>
to be the tail
of something
GOOD
than to be the head
of
nothing!

EDUCATION

is your

Best Friend

It
will
never
leave
You.

If you do not
practice

MEDITATION

You will
have to use

MEDICATION

Being a LEADER is like the SUN that gives light to the MOON and the EARTH.

良薦氣

Good

Humble
and
Honest

Spirit

Make your "GOOD" GREAT!

Then be humble
and realise that
your "GREAT" is only
GOOD!

Make new "GOOD" GREAT!

repeat the process...

Then move forward to
"GREATNESS"

希望

To **hope** is both
Mental and Physical

but

To have **faith** is
Mental, Physical and Spiritual

信仰

Don't dress

for the job that

you are doing

Dress

for the job

you want to do

or

the position

you want to be in.

Dress up...
Make up...
Move up...

It is

normal

to be successful...

it is

normal

to be rich...

anything else

is not

normal.

GOOD FORTUNE

We are...

one People

one Heart

One Destination

Keep your mind in your spine.

奥斯卡

Energy
is released
into the
organs
along the
spine.

Think upright

Think strong

Believe and...

... it will be so!

春 Spring

夏 Summer

秋 Autumn

冬 Winter

People
come into our lives
for a

Reason

a

Season

or a

Lifetime

The wise man builds his house upon ROCKS.

We must have a strong foundation!

Always go back and strengthen your basics.

The

Greatest

Leader

is

Inside

of

You!

THANK...

every part of your
body...

... to heal and
recover fully.

The
dialogue
you keep
with
negative
people
could
freeze
your
identity!!

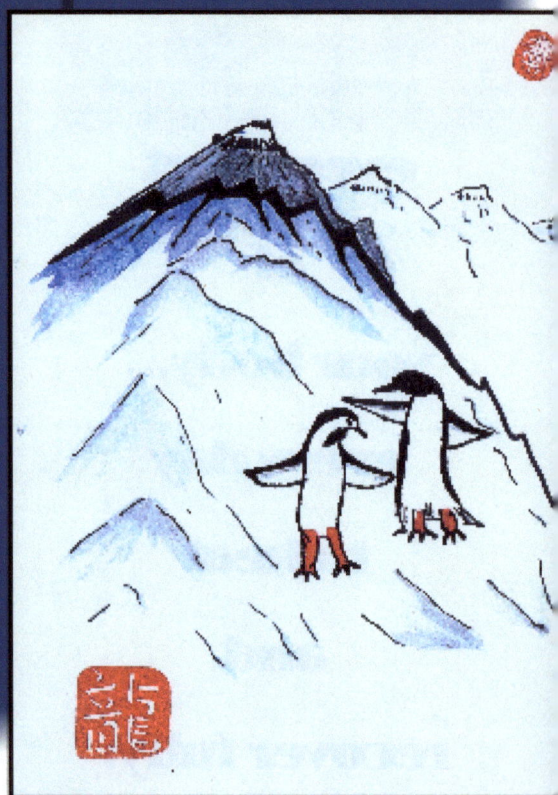

To understand the standard style...

You must carry the standard thought...

... and apply it everyday.

Everything

you want..

Wants

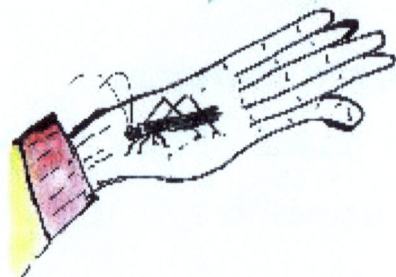

Something.

If you have a **Problem**

You will find a **Solution**

If you are willing to make a

Change

永遠愛 Lasting Love

富 愛

RICH LOVE

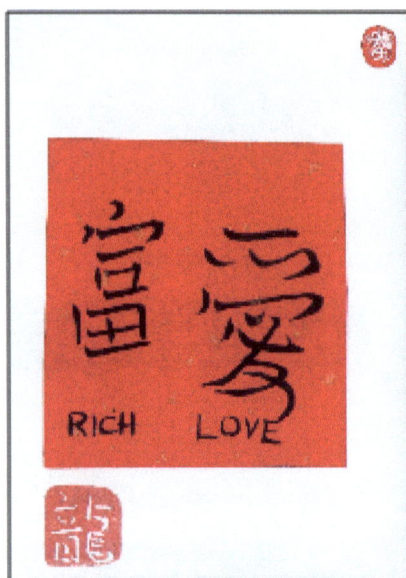

The longest journey is
the shortest distance.

It is between
the brain and the heart.

" The brain may think one thing
and the heart feels something
else"

The choice is
yours

Never **assume** that...

People are as

kind

thoughtful

considerate

and have great **integrity**

as you.

Be **kind** anyway...

Be **thoughtful** anyway...

Be **considerate** anyway...

Have great **integrity** anyway...

and success will always follow.

If the mind is strong, the body will be strong.

The body is the servant of the mind...

To re-condition the body we must re-condition the mind

The body will respond in like

so you can...

Heal thy self

The heights of

MADNESS

is doing the same things over and over again, expecting a different outcome.

A small change, will make a big

Difference

I will encourage

my friends

and

we will become brothers

and

together

we will greet this day

with truth

in our hearts.

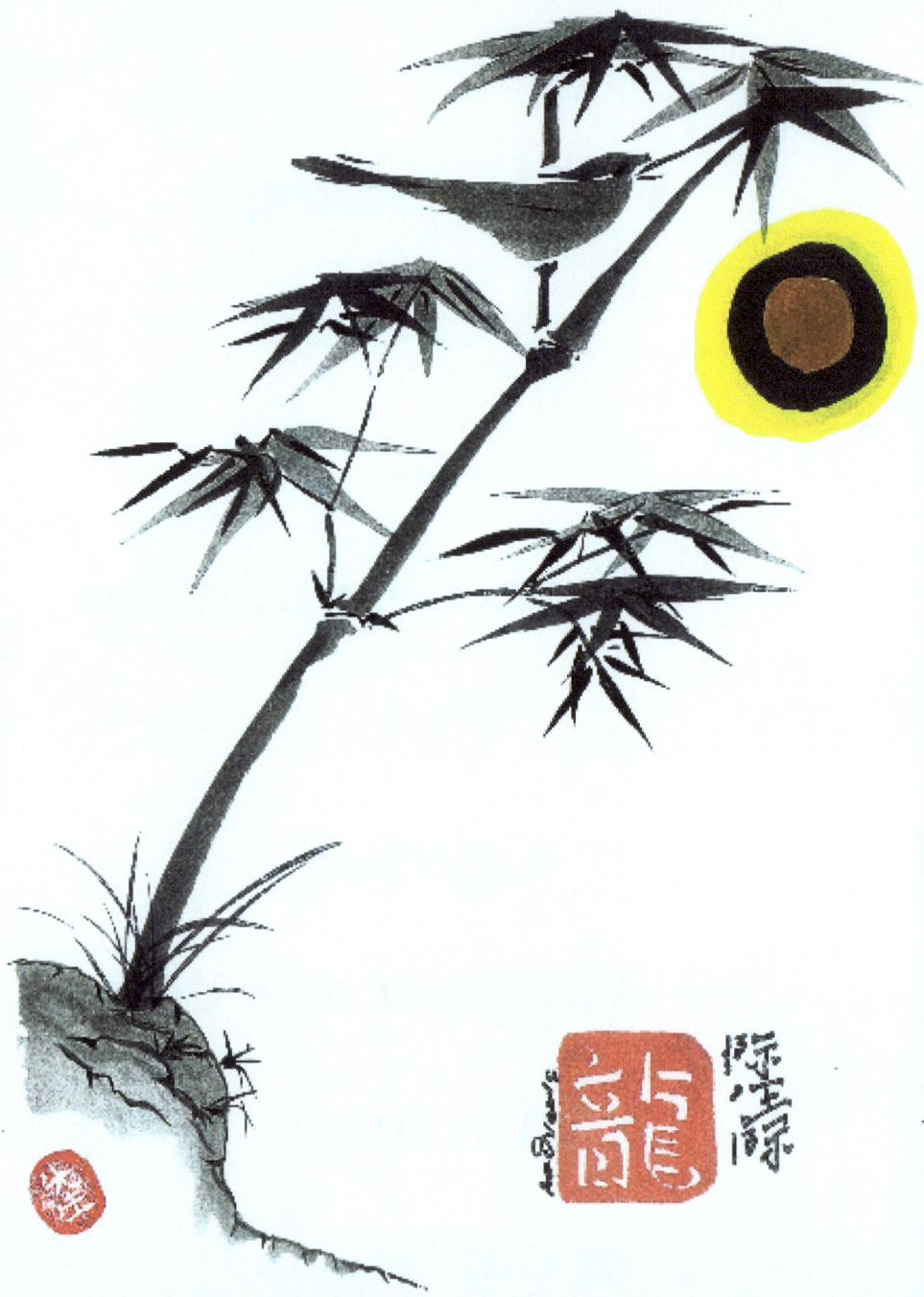

I will...

greet this day

with love in my heart

which is my

greatest weapon

and

none can defend

against it

Don Jitsu Form 2 Affirmation

My ability

will protect ME

when I am

alone

because

it is a plan

from

GOD

The Creator

Don Jitsu Form 4 Affirmation

Your BEST FRIEND is anyone who brings out the best in YOU.

To be a good LEADER you must first be a good FOLLOWER.

Lead by example
Lead by fitness not favoritism

Being alone is an opportunity to become A L L - O N E !

Mind

Body

Spirit

Emotions

Intellect

Ethereal

Connect with
the universal
energies

The seeds you plant could become the tree...

you must stand
under to recieve the
shade you need at
the time.

Sow...
seeds of love
and
seeds of prosperit

SOMETIMES... it is better to be
unched in the face by a friend...
Than to be kissed by an enemy.

A

BLESSING

means

To speak well of...

A

BLESSING

means

To do good for...

A

BLESSING

means

To think well of

YOU MUST USE YOUR
BLESSING TO IMPROVE
YOURSELF AND MOVE
UP IN LIFE.

IF YOU DON'T, THEN YOUR
BLESSING MAY BECOME
YOUR CURSE.

LOYALTY

is
un-swaying devotion
even when
the odds are
against
YOU!

KI-AI

(battle cry)

means

To draw out of one's self
an inner power
or inner strength.

It should feel as though
you are accompanied by a
powerful friend
who is always with you.

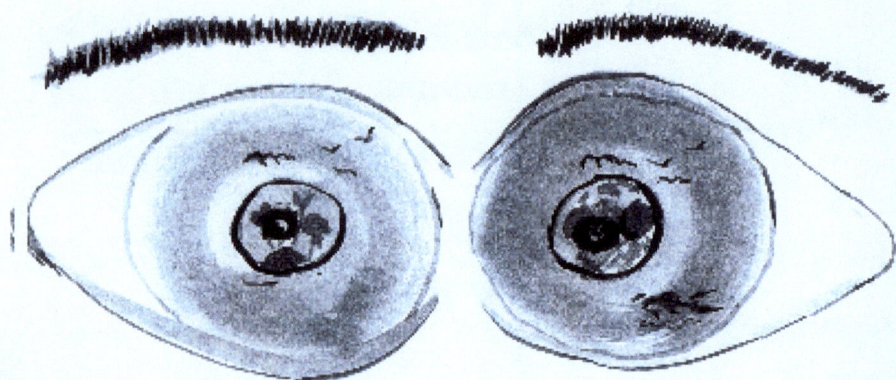

Never be afraid to look

into the eyes of LIFE.

To master

one's emotions

is a most rewarding

victory.

For others will test this

strength by trying to take

away your mastery

and

beat you up.

Sensei Albert A. Andrews

Determination

is like
a raging fire,
but when fueled by

ENTHUSIASM

one becomes

The UNSTOPPABLE FORCE

www.ingramcontent.com/pod-product-compliance
Lightning Source LLC
Chambersburg PA
CBHW042130080426
42735CB00001B/38